W9-COR-047

My School Helpers

SCHOOL BUS DRIVERS

Cindy Klingel and Robert B. Noyed

The Rourke Press, Inc.
Vero Beach, Florida 32964

PHOTO CREDITS
© Flanagan Publishing Services/Romie Flanagan

We would like to thank the students and staff of Channing Memorial
School for their valuable assistance in producing this book.

Library of Congress Cataloging-in-Publication Data

Klingel, Cynthia Fitterer
    School bus drivers / Cindy Klingel, Robert B. Noyed.
        p. cm. — (My school helpers)
    Includes index.
    Summary: Describes a school bus driver's day, as he picks up his bus, checks
it out, and takes the children to and from school.
    ISBN 1-57103-329-7
    1. Bus drivers—Juvenile literature. 2. School buses—Juvenile literature. [1. Bus
drivers. 2. School buses. 3. Occupations.] I. Noyed, Robert B. II. Title.

HD8039.M8 K58 2001
371.8'72—dc21
                                                            99-059284
                                                            CIP

Printed in the USA

CONTENTS

About the Authors

Cindy Klingel has worked as a high school English teacher and an elementary teacher. She is currently the curriculum director for a Minnesota school district. Writing children's books is another way that continues her passion for sharing the written word with children. Cindy Klingel is a frequent visitor to the children's section of bookstores and enjoys spending time with her many friends, family, and two daughters.

Bob Noyed started his career as a newspaper reporter. Since then, he has worked in communications and public relations for more than fourteen years for a Minnesota school district. He enjoys writing books for children and finds that it brings a different feeling of challenge and accomplishment from other writing projects. He is an avid reader who also enjoys music, theater, travelling, and spending time with his wife, son, and daughter.

The person you know best at school is probably your teacher. But many other school helpers keep the school running. You may not know about all they do. Here are some of the many things your school bus driver does.

Who is the first person that most students see on their way to school? It is the bus driver. The bus driver has a very important job. She is responsible for getting all the students to school safely and on time.

The bus driver is a familiar friend to students.

Before leaving to pick up the students in the morning, the bus driver checks out her bus. She walks through the aisle to make sure the bus is clean. She checks the lights and other **equipment** on the bus. She needs to know that the bus is safe to drive.

The bus driver makes sure the mirrors on the bus are working.

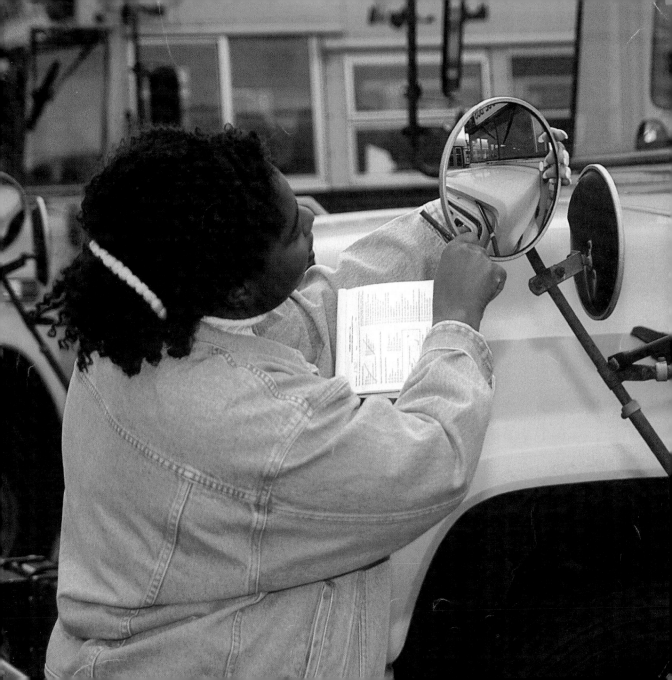

Once she knows the bus is ready, she leaves to pick up the students. Each bus driver has a **route** to follow. She knows where she needs to stop to pick up the students. She also needs to drive safely when driving on the country roads and city streets.

Bus drivers travel the same roads and streets every day.

She makes her first stop to pick up the students. When the bus stops, the lights flash on the bus. A stop sign on the bus tells other drivers to stop. Students then can safely cross the street to get on the bus.

All drivers must stop when the stop sign is put out.

The bus driver always greets the students as they get on the bus. The students enter the bus and find a seat. The bus driver waits until the students are seated. Then she is ready to go to the next bus stop.

A student gets on a school bus.

As the bus driver nears the end of her route, the bus is full of students. It is the bus driver's job to make sure the students stay seated in the bus. She helps the students understand the rules for riding the bus. This helps keep everyone safe.

Bus drivers are responsible for the safety of their riders.

The bus driver then drives the students to school. She stops in front of the school. She waits until all the students have left the bus. She now has another important job to do.

After the students arrive at school, the bus driver checks the bus.

Sometimes she drives students to their **field trips**. She picks up students at the school and takes them on their trip. It is fun for the bus driver to take students to interesting places. When the field trip is over, she brings the students back to the school.

Students sometimes travel on school buses during the school day.

The bus driver is now ready to bring the students home from school. She opens the door of the bus. The students come out of the school and get on the bus. It is time to go home.

After the last student gets off the bus, the bus driver's day is almost done. She brings the bus back to the **garage**. She checks the bus to make sure it is ready for the next day. Tomorrow will be another busy day for the bus driver.

Bus drivers bring their riders back home at the end of the day.

FURTHER INFOMATION

Books

Crews, Donald. *School Bus: For the Buses, the Riders, and the Watchers*. New York: Mulberry Press, 1993.

Flanagan, Alice K., and Christine Osinski. *Riding the School Bus with Mrs. Kramer*. Danbury, Conn.: Children's Press, 1998.

Hoban. Lillian. *Arthur's Back to School Day*. New York HarperCollins, 1996.

Web Sites
American School Directory,
http://www.asd.com/
Locate your own school's web site.

Kids, the School Bus, and YOU
http:.//www.ou.edu/oupd/schlbus.htm
Learn important traffic safety tips for riding the school bus.

A bus driver's day can be long.

GLOSSARY

equipment (ee KWIP ment) — tools

field trips (FEELD trips) — school trips to places such as museums, woods, or historical sites

garage (gar AHJ) — a building that protects cars or buses

route (ROOT) — the stops a bus driver makes every day

INDEX